Made in the USA
Las Vegas, NV
16 October 2024

96973769R00057